By
Arlyn Tolzmann

Illustrated By
The Tolzmann Brotherses

Illustrated by Matthew, Nathan, Peter, and Simon Tolzmann
Design by Nathan Tolzmann

ISBN 978-1-387-36318-6

Acknowledgments

Soli Deo Gloria

This book would apt
to have been scrapped
or trapped
on a hard drive,
more dead than alive,
without Nathan, Matthew, Simon, Peter,
also Jeanne, my edit leader.
Then Andrea and Emily,
two more in our family.
Their design
is divine;
their gifts from God
get my thanks and nod
for their art
full of heart.
It is true
through and through
they are a blest crew.
I thank others, too,
who help me do what I do.

Let all God's people say,
Hooray, hooray!

Jacob, while he traveled, needed a place to stay,
the accommodations he found weren't AAA.

With no hotel around,
his bed was the ground.

For a pillow he chose a stone,
in hopes he'd find the sleep zone.

He was so restless counting sheep;
somehow he managed to fall asleep.

Jacob dreamed of a ladder from heaven to earth,
with angels scampering up and down for all their worth.

The Lord introduced himself and then he spoke
'bout how Jacob's offspring would be a lotta folk.

No matter the direction he would face,
his offspring would be all over the place.

North, south, east or west,
his offspring would be blest.

Promised blessings the Lord would bestow
and to be with Jacob wherever he'd go.

Jacob awoke.
Jacob spoke.

In this very place where I speak and sit,
the Lord is here and I did not know it.

Awestruck, feelings of fear he could not douse,
for this was the gate of heaven, this was God's house.

The stone he slept on went from pillow to pillar;
he named the place, Bethel, which for him was a thriller.
Jacob then made this solemn vow:
if God clothes me and provides my chow,
if God is with me always, without cease,
and to my father's house I can go in peace,
then the Lord shall be my God,
my life's fulfiller,

I'll return a tithe and God's house will grow from this pillar.
To this day we're good at building to God's glory,
but the tithing part is quite another story!

Moses and the Burning Bush (Exodus 3:1-15)

Moses was working with his father-in-law's flock,
  no 9 to 5 job, but around the clock.

He led the sheep out in the boonies,
  morning, night and after-noonies.

Such a life made some loonies.
To the mountain called Horeb, he led,
  the sheep to another pasture to be fed.

An angel appeared out of thin air.
Yes, really out of nowhere.
An angel showed up in a bush on fire,
  so hot it made poor Moses perspire.

The fire burned, but not the bush,
  to find out why he would have to push.

God called to Moses, who kept ewe and ram,
  then Moses replied, here I am.

God said, take off the sandals from your feet
  and Moses must have wondered about the heat.

I do not want my feet medium well,
  to step back from the fire would seem just swell.

You are standing on holy ground.
A place of holiness you have found.
I am the God of your father and Abraham,
    the father of Isaac and Jacob, that I am.

Afraid to look at God in this place,
Moses covered up; he hid his face.
From Egypt I have heard my people's cries
    and the hope of freeing them on you lies.

You will deliver them to a good land
    where they in freedom will work and stand.

With my help you can do this, I have no doubt,
    you will go to Pharaoh and bring my people out.

How can I do this, little ole me?
How can I do this, set them free?
God said, I will be with you, you won't be alone.
I will be with you, you are my own.
It is I who send you by design and delight,
    with my freed people, you'll worship on this site.

Moses asked, what will I say is your name,
    for your people will ask, all the same?

I do not want to haw and hem,
    when asked, what will I tell them?
        Tell them I AM
        who I AM.
        Tell them I AM is the one who is sending
            and this is my name, I AM, never ending.
        Tell the children, the women and the men!
        Then wait to hear, their Amen! Amen!

Gideon (Judges 6:25-40)

Gideon's name on hotel Bibles appears,
yet he, like us, had plenty of fears.

The Lord spoke to him,
it was no whim;
down must come Baal's altar,
use a bull and do not falter.

Gideon would rather have just gone fishin',
than take on an idol-smashing mission.

Cut down the sacred pole;
it is your sacred role.

A new altar build,
then let a bull be grilled
over the chopped pole's fire.

It was the Lord's desire.

The altar belonged to his dad
and Gideon knew he'd be mad,
so he did the deed at night,
out of fear, out of sight.

The townsfolk were angry to the core,
they wanted blood to even the score.

Gideon found out
"to death" was their shout!

Despite their tirade,
his dad came to his aid,
and by heck,
he saved his neck.

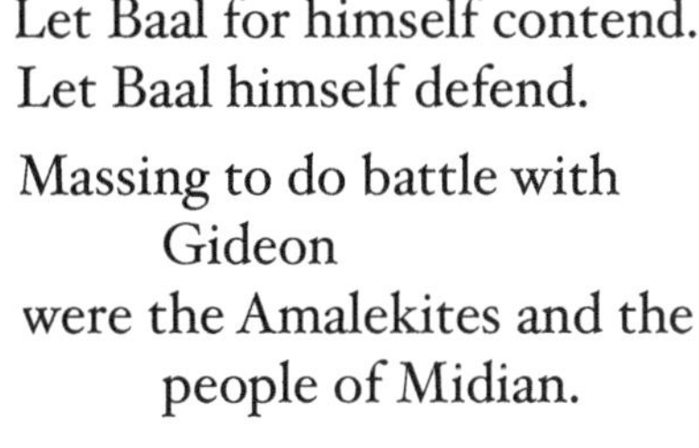

Let Baal for himself contend.
Let Baal himself defend.

Massing to do battle with
Gideon
were the Amalekites and the
people of Midian.

If Gideon had been heading to Oz for spyin',
    he would have hidden behind the cowardly lion.

Before he'd enter a fighting contest
    this uncertain one came up with a test.

God, how about turning the river to blood
    or creating a heap of butterscotch mud?

Or like Moses send hoards of frogs and gnats,
    or send in daylight a swarm of blue bats.

Gideon's plan was with fleece as white as snow,
    all God would need to do is put on a show.

How about at night put fleece on dry ground
    but in the morning, soaking, it is found?

Pull that one off and you'll be my buddy,
    in your hand, O Lord, I will be like putty.

God did it, yes mam,
    and it was no scam.

But Gideon would need more proof,
    that this was no trick or a spoof.

He had another plan with fleece, I do not lie;
    all God would need to do with it was only keep it dry.

And God did it, yes sir,
God is great we concur!
Our response is yippee Wowsers,
    from our hats to our hippy trousers!

If Gideon had a little lamb,
    its fleece as white as snow,
        after all the tests for God,
            the lamb's now bald, you know.

With no more tests up Gideon's sleeve,
    off to battle he now would leave.

Elkanah had two wives, Hannah was one.
His other wife had children, Hannah had none.
Hannah was ridiculed, she would weep and weep.
She was faithful to the Lord, but her pain was deep.
In the Lord's house she prayed and prayed
    that into a mother she would be made.

She wanted a son,
    only one.

The way her lips moved, she appeared to be drunk,
    at least that's what priest Eli, thunk.

No sir, my lord, I'm terribly vexed;
I'm troubled and don't know what to do next.
Eli saw her grief, saw her condition,
    and said to her, God grant your petition.

Hannah the believer
    became Hannah the conceiver.

She birthed Samuel, a son,
    and with joy was overcome.

When the boy, she did wean,
    at the Lord's house she was seen.

In gratitude she came up with this option,
Samuel would be the Lord's by adoption.
To the Lord, Samuel would always belong
    as she prayed words that one day would be Mary's song.

The bows of the mighty would be broken.
These were words that she had spoken.
The full would hire themselves out for bread,
    while the hungry would find themselves fed.

The poor would be raised from the dust;
    to this the rich would have to adjust.

Meanwhile, Eli's sons were evil and wicked,
    they messed with offerings and the folks were tick-ed.

When Hannah and Elkanah went to sacrifice each year,
Eli told them the Lord will give more children to rear.

It happened!
It happened!
Five times it was go!
Five times it was so!

A man of God told Eli his sons would die,
both on the same day, he did not lie.

God would raise up a new priest,
for Eli's sons were surely the least.

His family would have a tough life,
filled with hunger, filled with strife.

The Lord wasn't talking much in those days
and blessings were rare; God did not them raise.

Eli's eyes drew dim, he was in the dark,
as Samuel rested in the temple by the ark.

The Lord spoke, "Samuel, Samuel" with a voice,
breaking the long silence was the good Lord's choice.

Here I am, Samuel to Eli, said,
I heard your call, here I was led.
The third time this happened Samuel was told
to call out that he was a listening servant most bold.

Not one word the Lord said was for Eli good news,
not one word any of us to hear would choose.

The next morning when Samuel had awoken,
Eli asked him what the Lord had spoken.

Samuel laid it on him; he did, he did.
Nothing from Eli; he hid, he hid.
Samuel grew up, none of his words fell to the ground;
he was a trusty prophet, the people soon found.

There is much more to Samuel and his call,
how one day he anointed the king, named Saul.

Later he anointed David as king,
a feat that was no small thing.

Samuel then died, but did not have long to rest,
a medium brought him back at Saul's request.

Not one word Samuel said was for Saul good news,
not one word any of us to hear would choose.

His words from the grave overwhelmed Saul with fear,
they were Samuel's last words anyone would hear.

Nathan and David (2 Samuel 12)

David's romp with Bathsheba, he could not hide
and soon the prophet Nathan would him chide.
in no way with David was God a happy God
because of the king's lust for Bathsheba's bod.

David then saw to it her husband was killed,
this despicable act left God not thrilled.

Nathan told of two men, one rich, one not,
and before long David would be caught.

The poor man raised one little ewe;
like one of his children it grew.

How sweet his baahs,
the oohs, and the ahhs.

The rich guy had a whole flock of sheep.
The poor guy hand only one lamb in his keep.
The rich guy had a guest at his house
so he killed the lamb for din-din. What a louse!

David, when he heard this was hopping mad;
how could the rich guy be so bad, so bad?

The man deserves death, railed the king,
which from his mouth had a most hollow ring.

Nathan asked, you want the man to die?
Hear this o guilty one, you are the guy!

David had been very very naughty,
    now he was very very caughty.

David had lusted,
David was busted.
You are king, God gave you all,
    yet you caved to evil's call.

Your house will now see abundant trouble.
One day in shambles, it will be mere stubble.
What you did in secret and tried to hide
    will come to light to be known far and wide.

David, guilty as sin,
    to God turned himself in.

We want this to end, happy and good,
    like most fairy-tales of childhood would.

I'm sorry to say,
    the answer is nay.

Though much fasting and pleading were tried,
David and Bathsheba's baby died.
That's a tough one, a real bummer,
    more winter, than summer.

Life can have rough days without reason or rhyme,
    but with us our Lord will be each time.

Ahasuerus was also known as Xerxes,
the latter will suffice, we can say it with more ease.

Xerxes the king threw a huge feast,
it was for all, the great and the least.

This was a time his wealth he could show,
a time of luxury, to let the wine flow.

It was hearty, hearty,
party, party,
from the end to the starty.

Tipsy with wine the king called for his wife,
but she declined, which caused a lot of strife.

Maybe it was the queen's hurried ad lib,
maybe it was the start of women's lib.

This was not the way of a queen,
thus she was banned, not again to be seen.

A hunt for a new queen soon began;
beautiful and virgin was the plan.

One candidate was the daughter of Mordecai,
a Jewess she was and very easy on the eye.

The king's trusted eunuch did suggest her
and that's how the queen chosen was Esther.

Kings trusted eunuchs for one very good reason,
they were safe around women, no matter the season.

With Esther, the king was smitten down to his shoes
and he gave a banquet to spread this good news.

Then he promoted Haman to be his number one,
who was above all others, by decree it was done.

When subjects saw Haman they bowed on the spot,
but Mordecai, a Jew, refused, he would not.

Haman was mad, as mad as could be,
so he planned a dastardly killing spree.

It would be icky, it would be yucky,
the fate of the Jews would not be lucky.

A pur, or lot, was cast to decide the day
when the Jews would be killed without delay.

The king signed off on the dirty deed,
it would be law when the king decreed.

Mordecai heard it and put on sackcloth and ash;
to many the act seemed foolish and brash.

He said no to the clothes the queen had sent,
but on making a statement he was bent.

He would not,
could not,
give in one teeny tiny bit,
and no way would he just sit.

Esther asked the king to invite Haman to dinner.
This crafty wise woman had planned a big winner.

Haman was happy,
as happy could be,
until he saw Mordecai at the king's gate
and his stomach churned with what he just ate.

Haman ordered tall gallows to be built
on which to hang Mordecai, no matter his guilt.

At the banquet with Haman and the king,
Esther told how to life she and others would cling.
Who is the monster who would do such a thing?
"Haman," the queen answered and soon he would swing.
Because Haman had been hateful, such a louse,
Mordecai was given power over his house.
The king was asked to reverse his former decree
to kill all the Jews, as far as one could see.

So it was Esther saved her people from death's fray
and Purim is still celebrated to this very day.

The Book of Esther made quite the impact,
though God is not mentioned and that is the fact.

Elijah, the Faint-Hearted (1 Kings 19:1-21)

Of all the prophets, he is number one;
greater than Elijah, there is none.

All Baal's prophets were killed in a showdown;
the news of their demise spread quickly through town.

Queen Jezebel put a price on his head
and Elijah was just as good as dead.

He was one scared wreck,
she was out for his neck.

If Jezzie had her pick,
she'd have his head on a stick.

He would be an Elijahsicle,
for he was in quite a pickle.

His life was not worth a plug nickel or shekel,
this had gone way beyond a mere heckle.

Hell hath no fury like a queen scorned,
thus by a messenger, Elijah was warned.

He wanted to die when the going got rough,
he prayed to God that he'd had enough!

I would rather be cold dead
than to Jezebel lose my head.

Take my life and let it be
over and completely free.

Soon asleep, an angel woke him up
to tell him to eat and drink the cup.

It was heavenly, this angel bake,
thus the first angel food cake.

Again on the ground, he was a heap.
Again on the ground, he made not a peep.
Again on the ground he was asleep.
Awakened by the angel, you know the drill,
Elijah ate and drank, then had his fill.
Off he went, his own life to save;
he ended up hiding in a cave.

To a safe place, named Horeb, he ran,
thus he became a prophet cave man.

What are you doing here? the Lord spoke.
This was serious stuff, it was no joke!
It sounded mighty familiar, not at all odd,
    like the question to Adam and Eve, hiding from God.

Gee willickers, Lord, it's just you and me,
    all the other prophets are dead, you see.

I'm the only one left in the game.
I'm the only one left, what a shame!
Go stand on the mountain, the Lord will pass by.
Go stand on the mountain, give it a try.
Wind, earthquake and fire put on a show,
    but God was not there, don't you know.

After the violence
    came the silence,
        when Elijah appeared with mantle over his face,

God asked again, what are you doing in this place?
O Lord, I'm all bereft,
O Lord, I'm all that's left.
The Lord must have rolled the eyes
    when Elijah began to soliloquize.

I've heard enough,
    get off your duff!

There are kings and Elisha to anoint,
    go in the direction that I point.

That's when the story gets R-rated billing
    for all the fighting and the killing.

And there are 7,000 faithful, by the way;
Elijah, you are not alone, as you say.
Facing his fears, off he went,
    facing his fears, he was sent.

Follow his story, no longer the wimp he went around,
    he stood against evil and he did many astound.

How could he be the Messiah forerunner?
We say with scorn.
Then again,
    who expected the Messiah to be stable born?

On a chariot of fire ascended Elijah,
while down below, "Father" shouted Elisha.

It was an ancient street rod
built by the mighty Lord God.

It was an awesome scene,
if you know what I mean.

When the chariot was out of view,
Elisha tore his clothes in two.
He focused on God, he would not go off it.
With Elijah gone, he was the go-to prophet.
He picked up Elijah's mantle from the ground,
for the bank of the Jordan he was bound.

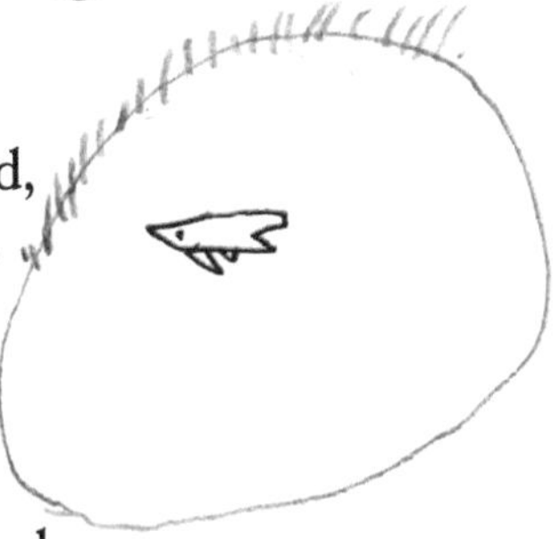

Elisha wasted no time
in doing the sublime.

A regular Moses at the Red Sea,
he parted the Jordan, and that's what they be.

Where is the Lord? he cried out.
Where is Elijah's God? was his shout.
Next a whole company of prophets came,
to say his spirit and Elijah's were the same.

They wondered if from his chariot he was thrown,
that might have happened for all they had known.

Maybe he was catapulted into some valley.
Maybe he was jettisoned into some alley.
Some made their pitch
he was in a ditch.

Elisha thought them a bunch of loonies,
but soon a search team was off to the boonies.

When they failed to find him, then was heard, I told you so!
Didn't I tell you, didn't I say, do not go?
In Jericho, the land
was not grand;
it was unfruitful, the water bad,
when you saw it, you went, egad!

The Jericho Water Board tried its best,
    but the water quality flunked the test.

To bring the yucky water to a halt,
Elisha took out some kosher salt.
Into a spring, the salt was flung
    and from the spring, clean water sprung.

Little did he know,
    little did it show
        that later would come the water softener,
            thence salt would be used far more oftener.

Whether to add what followed, I debated,
    for young children might find it X-rated.

When the prophet left town some boys jeered him,
    had they known, they would have feared him.

Baldy, baldy, no head of hair,
    you're as bald as a yellow pear!

They taunted Elisha, baldy, baldy go away,
    so he cursed them and two she- bears entered the fray.

The prophet might have been mostly bald,
    but forty-two boys were then mostly mauled.

There was no bald is beautiful then,
    even though the bald were dutiful men.

There was no yack,
    there was no flak.

God made perfect heads all bare
    but all the rest he covered with hair.

It was serious, these jeers and curses,
    as were the writers of the Bible's verses.

The good, the bad, the ugly are noted,
    while events and stories are not sugar-coated.

That is the way it is, receive it or leave it.
That is the way it is, deny it or believe it.
Elidsha lived a good many years
    and he was heard by a good many ears.

Isaiah (Isaiah 6:1-9a)

With the year King Uzziah died,
Isaiah's call does coincide.
He said, I saw the Lord with my own eye,
    sitting on a throne lofty and high.

The hem of his robe the temple filled
    while seraphs above angelically milled.

Did you catch that? It was only the hem.
Did you catch that? It was quite the gem.
They had wings to cover their faces,
    their feet and with two became flying aces.

They called out what we know as the Sanctus,
    a heavenly song where our heartstrings yank us.

Holy, holy, holy is the Lord of hosts,
    the whole earth, your glory toasts!

The thresholds shook,
I took a look.
The place filled up with holy smoke.
It did, it did, I do not joke!
The first thing I said was , woe, woe, woe!
Or maybe it was, oh, oh, oh!

Holy cow!
Holy now!
Holy wow!

My lips are unclean, at that I have a knack,
    around me unclean people are out of whack.

My lips are full of nasty words and things.
Woe is me, when I see seraphs with wings!
A seraph flew with tongs and burning ember,
    touching my mouth, or so I remember.

It must have hurt, I must have shouted
    when my guilt and sins were thus outed.

Then I heard the Lord's voice saying,
    whom shall I send without delaying?

Then like a child, with hand wildly waving,
    here I am, send me, I was raving.

To me, who earlier had just said, woe,
    the Lord spoke clearly, it's time to go!

Jeremiah (Jeremiah 1:4-19)

With Jeremiah the Lord began communications
and appointed him prophet to all of the nations.

Lord, I'm only a boy, I don't know how to speak,
isn't there some other person you could seek?

God said, you sound like Moses, that "I can't speak" bit;
but it did not work for him, you have to admit.

Do not fear, I will be with you, that's my intent
and you will speak my words wherever you're sent.

Jeremiah, Jeremiah, you're more than a boy.
Jeremiah, Jeremiah, you'll be my envoy.
Jeremiah, Jeremiah, don't be a killjoy.
Jeremiah, Jeremiah, you're in my employ.

The Lord's hand touched my mouth then the Lord said,
I'll put words in there and into your head.
Over kingdoms and nations, the power I grant,
to destroy, overthrow, to build and to plant.

Jeremiah, what do you see?
Why, it's the branch of an olive tree.
Jeremiah, what visions do come forth?
A boiling pot tilting from the north.
The nations on the north will be up a tree
for their wickedness and their forsaking me.

They have turned away from my commands
to worship gods they made with their hands.

Do not before them break,
or that same road you will take.

I made you a city fortified against the land;
against kings, princes, priests and people you'll stand.

They will fight you and treat you like chopped liver,
but they will not win, for you I'll deliver.

Jeremiah spoke God's word, the way he thought best;
and the opposition to him never took rest.

When first called, Jeremiah gave "no, thank you" a try,
and knowing a prophet's life, we understand why.

Daniel (Daniel 6)

Interpreting dreams was part of Daniel's genius,
becoming the head president under King Darius.

Some did not like this Daniel at all,
so they plotted for Daniel's fall.

Because he was above reproach
they would need some devious approach.

They perspired,
they conspired,
they desired
to have Daniel expired.

The plan that they saw
was to make a new law.

All people were to pray to the king,
for thirty days it was the thing.

The king is good. The king is great.
I thank the king for the food I take.

Those who refused would be thrown in the lion's den,
it was the law signed by the king's own pen.

To fit their devilish plans and serve their needs,
the law would be like that of the Persians and Medes.

There were no loopholes, not a one,
it was all set, it was all done.

About the law, Daniel very well knew,
yet three times to God he prayed in plain view.

The king sought a way out, but found none,
the law of the Persians and Medes would be done.

Trouble was abrewin'.
Trouble was astewin'.
The king wished he had not signed the law
but it was one he could not withdraw.

The king said, let us see what your God will do;
then he added, may your God be with you.

Back home the king fasted,
    all night it lasted.

Into the royal bedroom the king did slink;
    that night he caught not even one wink.

At dawn to the den of lions he hurried
    to see the fate of Daniel, he scurried.

Did your God save you from the lion's tummy?
Or must I find a new partner for gin rummy?
O great king, live on forever.
The lion did not my head sever.
An angel made sure I was not hurt.
An angel made sure I was not dessert.
To see him alive made Darius glad,
    with Daniel's accusers he became quite mad.

Into the den with their families they were thrown,
    so they would reap what they had sown.

Then Darius, the Mede,
    once again decreed,

the God of Daniel they were to fear,
    it was that simple, it was that clear!

Wedding at Cana (John 2:1-11)

In the Gospel of John, this was the first sign,
    when Jesus turned some water into wine.

Some are uneasy about this because of the addicted,
    they would prefer wine turned into water depicted.

It was at a wedding in Cana of Galilee
    where Jesus and his disciples had gone happily.

Jesus attended the party, which was no crime;
    like you and me, he enjoyed a good time.

The mother of Jesus was also there
    and of a problem she became aware.

Mary went to her son
    saying, the wine is all done.

Yes, that is bad, as you discern,
    but woman, it's not our concern.

Hospitality was a big passion,
    to run out of wine turned faces ashen.

I know many faces might turn glum,
  but Mom, my hour has not yet come.

She said to the servants, do what he tells you,
  though the orders of Jesus were very few.

He saw six jars made of stone,
  just standing there empty and alone.

Twenty or thirty gallons, these jars were big,
  more than enough for a generous swig.

The jars with water were filled to the brim,
  the servants had followed the orders from him.

They drew out some wine for the steward to taste
  and off to the bridegroom, he went in haste,

Everyone serves the best wine first,
  when the guests were drunk they serve the worst.

This tastes like the best vintage wine,
I can't describe it, it's better than fine.
You have saved the best wine until now,
I am shocked, all I can say is WOW!
This is the best wine I've ever had,
  most of what I get is pretty bad.

This is something few could afford,
  but such is the way of our good Lord.

It was vintage Jesus we might say,
  vintage Jesus on that wedding day.

Our cups are filled to overflowing,
  the grace of the Lord on us bestowing.

This was the first sign, what a blast,
  of course the joy did not last.

Because of many factors,
  the Lord soon had his detractors.

To start a marriage, invite Jesus to attend;
  then together from that day, on him depend.

Wilderness Test (Luke 4:1-13)

From the Jordan, Jesus was Spirt-led
into the wilderness that was ahead.

Such a place, scary it could be,
if you've been there, that's a certainty.

This was no picnic with hot dog bun,
this was anything but a time of fun.

This was no picnic that he faced,
for tough tests he'd need to be braced.

This was no simple casual walk,
but Jesus versus the devil talk.

For forty days it did last,
during which Jesus did fast.

No manna,
no banana,
no munchies,
no crunchies,
no snacks,
no flapjacks,
no energy drink,
on hunger's brink.

The tempter pointed to a stone,
make it bread or maybe a scone.

The cunning of Jesus then was shown,
we do not live by bread alone.

Jesus, the first test had won,
the devil's score now was none.

The test was a breeze, victory won,
but the devil was not about to be done.

All kingdoms are at your bidding,
it's the truth, I am not kidding.

You will have power and all glory,
that is it, that is my story.

If you please,
    on your knees,
        worship me
            is my plea.

Jesus saw right through that bunk,
    the devil's offer just plain stunk.

Only the Lord God was to be worshiped,
    something the devil's mind must have skipped.

The score for Jesus now was two,
    the devil, zero, it is true.

At the top of the temple Jesus was put,
    but in his own mouth went the tempter's foot.

We have gone both near and far,
    prove to me, the Son of God you are.

Just take a leap; the angels will catch you,
    by God's command they will snatch you.

Nothing sore will need to be rubbed,
    not even one toe will be stubbed.

Such a deal,
    such appeal;
        just jump, you can do it,
            just jump, you'll live through it.

Do not put the Lord to the test,
Jesus again had done his best.
For the tempter, it was strike number three
    and he took off as fast as fast could be.

With flying colors, Jesus passed the tests that day,
    so can we, when someone tries to lead us astray.

Like Christ we have Scripture, to which we can turn,
    thus it is evil's allure we can spurn.

The Lord will not leave us all alone,
    from his promises this has been shown.

The Healings (Mark 1:40-45, Luke 17:11-19)

A leper begged Jesus while kneeling
    to make him clean and do a healing.

If asked if it was something he would choose,
Jesus did not the leper refuse.
The diseased one beseeched,
    to him Jesus reached,
        the man to touch,
            though no one did such.

Leper spelled backwards is repel,
    it must have been a life of pure hell.

This was rare, certainly not routine,
    that a leper somehow was made quite clean.

Say not a word, but go
    to the priest, yourself to show.

This was the way for the cleansing Moses commanded;
    this was the way for the cleansing Moses demanded.

Off he went
    without consent;
        he was not deterred
            to spread the good word;
                to proclaim it freely,
                    he did it really!

Wherever Jesus went he drew a crowd
    for the healed one proclaimed the Lord out loud.

Another time,
    another rhyme.

Jesus, ten lepers met
    and the stage was set.

Leprous ones called out leper as warning;
    it was all part of their public scorning.

To keep away from the clean they might meet,
    lepers walked the other side of the street.

Lepers kept away as they asked for mercy,
    for what they suffered was adversey.

Go and show yourselves to the priests.

WHAM! They were healed, ready for feasts.

    Only one praised God and turned on back.
    Only one had a thankful knack.
    Only one at the feet of Jesus prostrated.
    Only one true thankfulness illustrated.

Yeah Jesus, he's my man
    and of him I am a fan!

This grateful one some called a charlatan,
    this grateful one was a Samaritan.

The chances of a foreigner seen as a hero,
    were small indeed and almost zero.

Where in the world were the other nine?
Where were they who received the cleansing of mine?
Why did not any praise God and return?
Why only this foreigner, whom many do spurn?

Get up and go on your way,
    your faith has made you whole, I say!

We do not know what befell the nine,
    the ones who missed this holy sign.

Perhaps they praised God and gave thanks each day,
Perhaps they were more thankful and that we pray.

Beatitudes (Matthew 5:1-12)

The Sermon on the Mount,
Matthew five to seven, we count.
The crowds surged where he was at,
so up the mount he went, he sat.

Rabbis sat while they taught,
no one there gave it a thought.

Those present had various attitudes
when Jesus shared what we call the Beatitudes,

The poor in spiritual matters will be blest,
theirs is heaven's kingdom, it is the best!

Those who have lost a loved one will indeed mourn,
yet be blest with comfort, which would them adorn.

The meek, those who are God directed
are blest with the earth, their gift collected.

Those hungry for God and with God to be right,
will be blest with a feast which is a delight.

When mercy giving is where your mind is set,
then the blessing of mercy is what you'll get.

Those who have hearts that are pure
will be blest to see God, for sure.

Blest will be those known as peacemakers,
to be God's children, they will be takers.

To be blest when persecuted or reviled
is to most of us just crazy wild.

Lies may be said of us on Jesus' account,
any blessing in that we'd quickly discount.

When lies we blurt,
then lies will hurt!

That we are called right then to be glad
reminds us persecution is what prophets had.

We are blest by the Beatitudes
and we respond with gratitudes.

Jesus, the Stand-Up (Luke 6:41-42)

We study the Gospels, all curious.
We wrestle with Christ's teachings, most serious.
He was the master of the story,
    which he used to point to God's glory.

We fail to see him as humorous.
    though many times Christ does humor us.

We have clean glasses aplenty
    to help us see twenty - twenty.

Yet some things get in our way,
    like judging others each day.

We look hard and long
    to find in others some wrong.

We search like heck
    for some tiny speck,
        some sawdust in an eye,
            for sure I do not lie.

We peer all the while
    through our own woodpile.

Before you seek their specks and say, hot dog,
    look in the mirror at your own huge log.

Take that lumber out of your eye,
    say to it right now, good bye.

Those who heard Jesus say such,
    would have laughed and giggled much.

At times he was funny, I have no doubt,
    it is something good; I think we should shout.

Many times he used hyperbole
    to make his points most noblely.

If a funny Jesus doesn't fit our profile,
    then perhaps we could at least see his smile.

At worship with friends or kin
    we too, might sometimes pop a grin!

Jesus on Worry (Matthew 6:25-34)

If there's one place we like to hurry,
it is the place we call worry;
it's a part of our nature,
of that we are sure.

Worry is like having a toupee,
we'd rather not have one, we say.

It is what we've got,
though we'd rather not.

Our life can turn to disarray
when worry comes to rule our day.

Jesus said, don't worry about the life we'll meet,
about what we'll drink or what we'll eat;
about our body, what we'll wear,
or what in the world we'll do with our hair.

Look at the birds who are God fed,
if they were not, they'd surely be dead.

Birds do not shop at the grocery store,
God gives a banquet with foods galore.
When is the last time we saw birds plant a crop?
When is the last time we saw birds go shop?
Have you ever seen them start
to push a grocery cart?

Birds have their worth, like a gem,
    but your worth is far more than them.

By worrying can you add days to your life?
Or does worry cut life short, like a knife?
Think of all the worries you have about clothes,
    it's one way to drive yourself looney, I suppose.

You stand before mirrors to see how you look,
    without a thought of how long it took.

You worry and worry getting all uptight,
    then ask the question, do I look alright?

You worry and worry about getting old,
    the age you once were, you grab onto and hold.

Wise persons will say you just look fine,
    it is the smart answer that won't malign.

Look at the lilies of the world, how they grow;
    they don't knit or crochet and they do not sew.

Solomon in all his glory was not clothed like a lily,
    to say he was is untrue, just plain silly.

He might have had power, he might have had money,
    but compared to a lily, he would have looked funny.

If God clothes the grass which is alive this day
    and later it is burned, not made into hay;
        then God will clothe you, with an eye for design;
            it could be said this clothing is purely divine.

Stop worrying about what to drink, what to eat,
    what to wear and if medium rare should be meat.

The nations of the world strive for such things,
    whether belts match shoes and watches match rings,
        or worrying if tomorrow the fat lady sings.

To many such things the world clings,
    yet without faith, it's what worry brings.

Worry is the think seed
    that becomes stinkweed.

God knows what you need.
God knows it indeed.
If the kingdom strives and in God does dwell,
    then all else will be yours as well.

Have no fear little flock,
    the Lord God is your rock.

Have no worry, no qualms,
    sell what you have, give alms.

Make purses that will not wear out,
    store treasure in heaven, then set out;
        for in heaven, no moths or thieves can attack,
            or destroy or steal or treasure hijack.

This treasure will never corrode or rust
    or tank when the stock market does go bust.

It's God's grand pleasure
    to provide us a treasure,
        that holds firm against worrying
            and slows down our scurrying.

For wherever your treasure is, you see,
    that is where your heart will be!

The Woman Who Anoints Jesus (Luke 7:36-50)

Jesus and others sat down to eat
    when ointment was poured all over his feet.

All Gospels to a woman point,
    it's Mary, or a sinner who does anoint.

They do not agree whose house she was at,
    whose table it was where the good Lord sat.

I will let Luke have his say
    to tell what happened on that day.

Somehow a woman who had no appointment
    brought to a Pharisee's house a jar for anointment.

Behind Jesus she stood crying a bucket of tears,
    this act of humility did not bring on cheers.

His feet by her tears were washed,
    her act of love was not squashed.

How could she even dare
    to wipe his feet with her hair?

The woman was no winner.
The woman was a sinner.
She poured ointment, then kissed his feet,
    as the guests were seated to eat.

The host was taken aback
    by the woman's impulsive act.

Thus came a teachable time,
a moment sublime
for Jesus, a story to share
about forgiveness and God's care.

One debtor owed a whole lot,
the other debtor, not.

When neither could pay,
their creditor did say,
I forgive your debt,
it is all set.

Whose love will be the deeper?
Whose love will be the keeper?
The one forgiven most,
was the answer of the host.

Later Simon, the host,
received a bit of a roast,
for his lack of hospitality,
an obvious actuality.

Unlike this woman, my feet you did not wash.
Do you remember that? I do not josh.
You gave me no kiss,
  but she did not miss.

You did not anoint my feet with oil,
  she anointed them and did not recoil.

She used her hair as a dryer,
  that my friends you must admire!

Her sins were not just a few,
  there were old ones and some new.

The one forgiven much from above
  will be the one with the greater love.

The one who is forgiven little,
  is the one who loved just a piddle.

The one forgiven a heap
  will have the love more deep.

The woman got,
  right on the spot,
    a lesson taught,
      like it or not.

Jesus with a whole lot of nerve
  forgave her sins with great verve.

Those seated at the table,
  asked how Jesus was able
    to forgive her sins right there,
      or forgive anyone anywhere.

We do not sin that grace may abound,
  for grace is not far but always around.

While we were still sinners Christ died for us;
  that is the good news we share and discuss.

Faith saved her, in peace the woman went,
  she left the room in bewilderment.

This is the Gospel of the Lord.
Praise to Christ, let him be adored!

Lost Sheep (Luke 15:1-7)

Jesus surely knew it was coming
because of those with whom he was chumming.

The good pious ones who liked to point,
soon would find their noses out of joint

They leveled their many accusations
about those of dubious reputations.

This man eats his dinners
with all kinds of sinners!

What could be worse
or more perverse,
they grumbled
and mumbled.

What's with this guy?
Oh my, oh my!
The goody goodies
shouldy shouldies,
by Jesus were met,
and a parable they'd get.

Imagine you have one hundred sheep
and all of them are in your keep.

One sheep goes astray,
would you without delay,
leave the ninety-nine,
or would you sing auld lang syne?

You would search all around
until that sheep is found.

On your shoulders you'd lay it
and rejoice, you would say it.

Joyfully you would expound,
my sheep was lost and now is found!

Now my friends comes the scoop
    about the one who flew the coop.

In heaven the joy is great,
    each time our sins we state.

The partying in heaven far surpasses
    those who look through their righteous glasses.

Lost Coin (Luke 15:9-10)

Luke fifteen has three stories of the lost,
    these words are about coins and the cost.

The lost sheep and lost son choose to go,
    while the coin could not choose to do so.

A woman, ten coins she had,
    if one was lost she might feel sad,
        mad
            or bad.

The lamp she lit;
    she did not sit.

She did what most would do,
    she looked everywhere she knew;
        high and low,
            up on top and down below;
                every cranny, every nook,
                    she gave a very thorough look.

Up she lept,
    up she swept
        the whole house spic,
            the whole house slick,
                the whole house span
                    was the plan.

She was resigned,
    her coin to find.

Though at times it might look bleak,
    the coin would lose at hide-n-seek.

Sure enough, it was found,
    then came her "yippee!" sound.

After her search and labors,
    she called all her neighbors
        to come and rejoice,
            to give thanks with one voice.

Some might think her not a smarty
for what she spent on the party
that she had tossed
when she found what once was lost.

In heaven, what a sight,
that's right;
the joyful yelling,
the joyful telling
of the lady or gent
who comes to repent.

Luke fifteen is about the found,
how heaven does resound
in joyful exultation
at a sinner's reclamation.

That is good news we hear,
a love message most clear.

All heaven rejoices when we turn around,
after being lost and then by God being found!

Amen! Amen! We go.
Amen! Amen! It's so!

Lazarus and the Rich Guy (Luke 16:19-31)

There was a rich guy,
vast riches piled high,
who dressed
the best
and ate that way
most every day.

A poor man, Lazarus, lay at his gate.
He could not recall the last time he ate.
The rich guy , to Lazarus; never opened his doors,
who wants to watch a man covered in sores?

If made folks feel queasy and sick
to watch the dogs, his sores did lick.
Ew!
P.U.!
Whew!

Some saw him as disgusting, I guess,
but when he died there was a regress.

To Abraham's side, angels carried him away;
then the rich guy had his own death day.

The guy was tormented in hell,
that's the story Jesus told so well.

For a mere drop of water the rich guy asked,
while Lazarus in sheer comfort basked.

The rich guy had luxury his whole life,
while Lazarus mostly had mucho strife.

The request was nixed,
  a chasm was fixed
    and there was no bridge to cross it that way,
      on one or the other side, souls would have to stay.

The rich guy begged, down on his knees,
  go warn my family, please, please, please!

The reply came, they have the prophets and Moses,
  they should listen to them, right under their noses.

Please, I know they'll repent,
  if someone from the dead is sent.

Abraham said,
  without Moses and the prophets in their head,
    they will not be convinced if one rises
    from the dead!

There is no guessin',
  this ends our lesson!

The Vineyard (Mark 12:1-12)

Jesus spoke in parable form,
    such a practice was often the norm.

A man planted a vineyard, added a fence,
    a wine press, and watchtower for defense.

No one would steal his grapes or wine
    while he was gone, all would be fine.

The tenants were left in charge,
    no small trust but very large.

The owner sent a slave to check things out,
    but the tenants beat and punched him in the snout.

Later slave number two was sent,
    but on more violence they were bent.

More slaves were sent as the owner willed,
    but they were beaten and some were killed.

Then he sent his much loved son,
    surely they would respect this one.

He soon learned this was a bad mistake
    and it turned into sad heartache.

They killed the son to get the vineyard,
    but they got not get even a shard.

No longer employed,
    they were destroyed.

It's the old story of the stone once rejected,
    that became the cornerstone erected.

When Jesus finished his parable gem,
    the goody-goodies knew it was about them.

Thus they planned on a Jesus arrest,
    but they stopped for fear of the crowd's protest.

They quietly sneaked out the back door,
    to try later to even the score.

With tails between their legs, they went away,
    for then they were in great disarray.

The Guy Who Wouldn't Forgive (Matthew 18:23-35)

A king forgives a huge debt of a slave,
not the normal way most kings behave.

That's nuts, that's crazy, by all rights,
but it is what Matthew writes.

You can't imagine what comes next
in the reading of the text.

When slave number one could not come up
with the gold,
with his wife and children he was to be sold.

Soon on his knees,
up went his pleas;
no, no, I will pay you back,
please, please cut me some slack!

Jesus enjoyed hyperbole,
a way to help folks to see
forsooth,
some truth.

One hundred fifty thousand years of work was his debt;
no more ridiculous could a parable get.

Those who heard Jesus must have laughed
or at least thought him to be a bit daft.

The begging and the king's heart did the trick,
the slave's debt was erased mighty quick.

Slave number one would become a gracious one,
    whose charity would never ever be outdone.

Sorry, my optimistic friends,
    that is not how the story ends.

Slave number one turned right around,
    and he refused to share the forgiveness he'd found.

Slave number two owed slave number one a small amount,
    every cent would need to be paid on his account.

Slave number one grabbed number two by the throat,
    pay up, or else. That you can quote!

Slave two begged for time, to no avail,
    so slave one had two thrown in jail.

How dare he cause such a scene?
How could he be so very mean?
It makes us so mad we want to spit,
    or at least throw some kind of fit.

We voice our fury,
    put us on his jury!

The king was told what had been done,
    how slave one's mercy added up to none.

Since mercy is what slave one refused to share,
    the king took back his mercy, which seemed fair.

Mercy received is not just to celebrate;
    showing mercy to others is our mandate.

Zacchaeus (Luke 19:1-10)

It's not easy being short,
    or so some persons report.

How would you like to be
    known as the shrimp up a tree?

There was a tax man, Zacchaeus,
    whose story should not flee us.

Of the tax guys, he was the chief,
    to some that meant he was a thief.

Through Jericho Jesus was passing,
    while quite the crowd was amassing.

Zacchaeus couldn't see because he was short,
    thus he had to climb a tree as a last resort.

There he was, up a sycamore tree,
    high above all. to see what he could see.

When Jesus came to the place,
he quickly cut to the chase.

Jesus, a man of considerable renown,
called to Zacchaeus, to come on down.

I want to stay
at your house today.

It's as simple as that,
I want to chat.

Down the tree he came real snappy,
to welcome Jesus he was most happy.

The bystanders grumbled.
the bystanders mumbled,

Jesus has gone to be a guest
of a sinner, who is a pest.

How could he even enter the house
of a tax guy, that little louse?

Zacchaeus promised the Lord that day
to the poor he'd give his stuff away.

I will give back four times as much to those I defrauded,
now this was good news and Jesus applauded.

To this house salvation came as Abraham's son,
since the Lord spoke those words, it was surely done.

This must have come as a big surprise
and must have opened a lot of eyes.

For Jesus came to seek and save the lost,
no matter, no matter what the cost.

From sin, from death, Jesus frees us,
even the likes of the scorned Zacchaeus.

It is as plain as plain can be,
Jesus saves both you and me.

He does, he does,
as it is, as it was!

Sheep and Goats (Matthew 25:31-46)

Parables are like a knuckleball,
    they surely aren't one size fits all.

We think we have them figured out,
    then they jump and do a turnabout.

Jesus was master of this story form,
    though at times they caused quite the storm.

Parables twist, parables turn,
    parables teach us as we learn.

They faze us,
    they amaze us,
        they make us wink,
            they make us think.

When Jesus taught of judgment day,
    here is what he had to say.

All people will line up before the king,
    to his kingdom invite they will cling.

Listen people, do take notes,
    we are talking sheep and talking goats.

Goats to the left, just stand tight;
    sheep line up on my right.

You fed me when hungry, that came first.
Drink you gave me to quench my thirst.
A stranger, you set out the welcome mat.
Naked, you clothed me from shoes to my hat.
I was sickly and to my house you came.
In prison, you did not scold me, you did not shame.

After baa, baa, the sheep will say,
    when did we do this anyway?

The king will say,
    without delay,
        as you served others, I ask you to see,
            you did all of these things also to me.

To those on the left, the king showed the door,
wait just a minute we want to hear more!

Fair enough, the king said,
but you'll not be spoon fed.

I was hungry, as hungry can be;
all you did was stuff yourself in front of me.

For me, not a bite,
for me, not a mite.

My tongue was parched like a desert so dry
and with your super-sized drink, you walked on by.

A stranger, you ignored me,
you just did not see.

Naked, you had me arrested as a flasher.
Some hand-me-down clothes would have been less rasher.

I was sick, feeling nearly half dead
you were too busy to visit you said.

Imprisoned, you were embarrassed I was in that place,
so for years and years not once did you show your face.

Wait, wait, that is not true;
In such we never saw you!

The king replied, you are so very right,
you missed me in them, you had no sight.

If you are one who is mostly greedy,
you will never see me in the needy.

That is it with goats and sheep,
some are happy, others weep.

The Demoniac (Mark 5:1-20)

In the land of the Gerasenes, Jesus exited the boat
    and was met by a madman we note.

He lived in a cemetery mostly,
    all alone, an existence most ghostly.

He couldn't be restrained by shackle or chain,
    no one dared to go near him; he was insane.

Day and night he scowled.
Day and night he howled.
Day and night he growled.
Day and night he prowled.

It was a wonder he didn't break bones,
    as he struck himself with the stones.

What a sight, to Jesus he ran!
I would have run away as fast as I can.

Before Jesus he bowed,
    then he shouted aloud.

What, Son of God, have you to do with me?
By God, do not torment me is my plea!

Come out of the man, you unclean spirit,
    said Jesus, who made sure he could hear it.

Jesus asked the man, what is your name?
He always wants to know us, that is no game.
Legion, he said, because of the spirits unclean.
Please send them all to some far away scene!

On a nearby hill
    swine ate their swill.

We could say pigs, instead of swine,
    that to many would be just fine.

The spirits begged and pleaded,
    for a new home they needed;
        maybe our new digs,
            could be in those pigs.

The Lord said, okay,
    so they headed for the bay.

There must have been one cacophonous sound
    as two thousand pigs in the sea were drowned.

Imagine the squeals and snorts,
    imagine the sounds of all sorts!

The swineherds ran, scared half to death,
    to tell what happened, all out of breath.

The curious townsfolk came out to see
    the demoniac now dressed, calm as could be.

Now they were scared
    and to Jesus they declared,
        it would be good
            if you left our hood.

The man who was healed,
    to Jesus appealed,
        with you I want to go,
            whether high, whether low
                but the answer was no.

Go home to tell your tale,
    while the Lord's mercy you hail.

Tell what the Lord has done,
    the wholeness gift you've won.

The man was content,
    so to the Ten Cities he went
        to tell his story
            and give God the glory.

The man who once was crazed,
    now the crowds he amazed.

Such is the story of Legion's horde,
    how to ministry he was called by the Lord.

What do we learn from the demoniac text?
God's call to new service, we may be next!

On the Lord's resurrection day
two were headed on their way
out of town,
a bit down.

It's difficult to conceive
that they decided to leave.

They discussed what in Jerusalem had taken place.
While they chatted, Jesus joined in
their walking pace.

They did not recognize Jesus by their side,
as he questioned them, as he walked astride.

Both looking sad, in their tracks stopped dead,
we thought the news of Jesus was wide spread.

He was mighty in word and deed.
He was mighty with those in need.
He was gracious with the doubters.

He was gracious with the outers.

The chief priests and leaders put him to death,
    he hung on a cross til his very last breath.

He had helped us cope.
He had helped us hope.

Some women astounded,
    some women confounded
        us that Jesus was alive, not dead.

Honestly, that is what they said!

We are truth tellers
    and honest fellers.

We do not lie,
    oh my, oh my!
Sure enough, they went to the tomb
    only to discover an empty room.

How foolish you two are, Jesus declared,
    this is what the prophets of old had shared.

The Messiah would suffer, then enter his glory.
The tomb was only his brief dormitory.

The scriptures at once Jesus began to unfold,
    in hopes the truth about himself they'd behold.

As the village of Emmaus drew near,
Jesus shifted his pace into high gear.

They said stay with us, please don't go,
    soon it will be dark, don't you know?

So it was, leaving was delayed.
So it was, the Lord Jesus stayed.
So it was, he blest and broke the bread.
So it was the two were fed.

In an instant, with eyes open wide,
    they must have sat mystified;
        for Jesus had vanished from their sight,

Jesus had vanished into the night.

They said, on the road our hearts were burning,
while the scriptures we were learning.
Off to Jerusalem was their intent.
Off to Jerusalem the two then went.
The women were right, their words we should heed.
The Lord has risen, he has risen indeed!

Their joyous excitement they showed,
telling what took place on the road.

Jesus became known in the way they were fed.
Jesus became known in the breaking of bread.

Then just like that, in their midst he stood;
he terrified them and startled them good.

They thought we was a ghost.
They thought they were toast.

He showed them his hands and feet,
then he asked for something to eat.

Where they gathered to share their grieving,
now was joyful mixed with disbelieving.

With the scriptures he opened their minds,
new insights were formed of all kinds.

Now that you have seen me with your own eye,
wait for the power to come from on high.

Repentance and forgiveness through his holy name;
they were called to share and called to proclaim.

To Bethany the disciples went, they had not tarried
and Jesus blest, then to heaven he was carried.

They worshiped the Lord, they were not coy
and into the temple they blest God with great joy.

Baptism of the Ethiopian (Acts 8:26-39)

The angel told Philip, go south young man,
so he packed up as fast as fast can.

The road was no stroll in the park,
it was a wilderness quite stark.

There was a certain eunuch,
now don't say ew yuck!

Since this poem is G-rated,
no definition is slated.

Suffice it to say, that around the queen,
the eunuch as harmless by the king would be seen.

His was a very important job
and with the elite he could hob nob.

He oversaw the treasury of the queen,
but soon ensued a remarkable scene.

In Jerusalem he had gone to worship
and now he headed home on his return trip.

In his chariot, he tried Isaiah to read,
but to interpret it, some help he would need.

Philip was nudged by the Spirit that day
as he overheard the eunuch read away.

The next thing Philip knew,
he had joined the retinue.

He interpreted the text on sheep,
which the eunuch found too deep.

He asked about whom the prophet spoke,
was it himself or some other folk?

Philip told of Jesus, which was good news,
it was exactly what the eunuch could use.

Water was spied
by the roadside;
would Philip allow
his baptism right now?

Into the water they went
    and Philip on his way was sent.

The eunuch rode off rejoicing,
    his good news no doubt voicing.

Out of nowhere God can appear.
Out of nowhere God can draw near.
Out of nowhere God can be here.

Cornelius and Peter (Acts 10)

There once was a man named Cornelius,
  who had a vision most serious.

That sounds like a limerick start,
  but from that idea we'll depart.

By an angel, his prayers and giving were noted.
Send me to Joppa to meet Peter, was quoted.
This we read in Acts verse ten,
  of what happened way back then.

At noon the very next day,
Peter went to a roof to pray.
He was hungry and needed something to eat.
He fell into a trance and saw a large sheet.
In it were creatures of every kind,
  when told to kill and eat, he declined.

I've never eaten what is unclean and profane,
  to do such now Lord would be insane.

What God has made is not profane, was voiced
  and soon to heaven the sheet was hoist.

The men arrived to ask Peter to come their way,
  so Cornelius could hear what he had to say.

They were sent,
    so Peter went,
        he did,
            he did,
                I do not kid.

When Cornelius saw him, he fell at his feet,
    he thought him a god, thus the way to greet.

No, no, I'm just a man,
    is the way Peter began.

In a Gentile house you wouldn't find a Jew,
    for such a thing was unlawful to do.

God showed me what God makes is always good,
    that's why I'm in this place, in your hood.

God plays no favorites, wherever you're from;
    to those who follow and do right, he says come.

God anointed Jesus with the Spirit, with might,
God was with him to do good and heal alright.

Then they hung him on a tree
    until he was as dead as could be.

Then God raised him from the dead,
    this good news we are called to spread.

God ordained him to judge the living and dead,
    which is why we have not a thing to dread.

Believe in him, call out his name,
    forgiveness to all is his aim.

Sound far-fetched?
Let it be etched
    forever on your heart and your mind,

God is the lover of all humankind.
Peter called for Gentiles to be baptized,
later for that he would be chastized.

All of this inclusion from a vision he had
    and for that to this day, give thanks and be glad!

Do Not Judge Matthew (7:1-5, Luke 18:9-14)

At times we feel so right,
we are quick to indite
the ones we see as lesser
and it does not take a guesser
to crow it,
show it,
know it,
and blow it.
We are the winners;
they are the sinners.
We win,
we're in,
they're out,
we shout!
Look at me,
look and see
how good I am,
it is no sham,
how great I am,
I am!

Look how high we set the bar,
look how low those others are!
Jesus was direct,
Jesus was correct,
which is nothing new
for me, for you.

Before you peck
at the speck
in another's eye,
eat humble pie;
for how can you see
with what seems a tree
stuck in your own
as it is shown?

Look first at your own sin,
the mess you're in.

Or recall the pharisee so right,
the one so full of spite,
the one so brash
he called the tax man trash.

Full of his pride, full to the brim,
he was thankful to be unlike him.

He is morally weak,
an immoral freak.

To be like me, others should seek,
for I fast two times a week.

I tithe my income,
a most tidy sum,
unlike this back row scum,
this tax collector bum.

The tax man's heart and head bowed
as he pleaded for mercy out loud;
he beat his chest
as he confessed.

The tax man faced his own scorn,
the other blew his own horn.

One was about me, myself and I,
as he looked down on the other guy;
he was self-pleased, self-satisfied,
the other by God was justified.

The exalted were humbled,
no doubt as they grumbled,
while the humbled drew nigh
and were exalted on high.
Ours should be a solemn oath
to help others in their growth;
to pray, Lord keep our eyes on you,
not on those about whom we stew.

To judge others brews discontent,
to love and accept brings our content.

Once again the Lord's surprise exists,
as his word turns us and then it twists.

The Great I Am (from John's Gospel)

Way back in Moses' time,
    long before yours, long before mine,
        he wanted, when shove came to push,
            the name of the one in the burning bush.

I Am is what he heard,
    that's what came by God's word;
        I am
        who I am.

It was as simple as that,
I am came from a chat.

This was no name pulled from a hat.
    I am would do as God stood pat.

Jesus used I am many a time,
    long after people wrote in rhyme.

By I am, a tie to God he would make,
    which caused many a head to shake.

When Jesus chose I am to use,
    for some it was an explosive's fuse.

Before Abraham,
    Jesus said, I am.

They picked up stones to throw
    at him for this blatant show.

How could he be one with God?
Thus be became a lightning rod.
How could he be one with God?
This seemed to them mighty odd.

I am the bread of life, no mere slice,
    far more than enough to suffice.

The I am gives what will last,
    while the world offers what is fast.

A crowd was hungry for a meal,
    with no coupons they still got a deal.

At least five thousand were fed,
    with some fish, with some bread.

Sir, give us the heavenly bread,
    it was what they asked, what they said.

To the ones who were the underfed,
Jesus answered, I am the living bread.
How could this be?
We just don't see.
We know his Mom and Dad.
He must be bonkers mad!

Eat of my flesh, you will have life;
    these Jesus words caused more strife.

It all started with the I am
and soon it turned to real bedlam.

To those who lived in darkness, much like night,

Jesus spoke openly, I am the light.

Yes, he is bright.
Yes, he is right.
Yes, he is light.
Yes, his insight.

The world was dark,
was his remark;
they needed the divine
on them to shine.

But I am was so much more
to praise, worship and adore.
The I am is resurrection, truth, life and way,
good shepherd and gate day after day.

The I am is also the true vine,
as branches he says you are mine.

I am is in bread, I am is in wine,
when I am is with us together we shine.

On the night of his arrest,
the I am did his best
to tell them who he was
amidst the darkness and buzz.

Are you Jesus of Nazareth place?
I am, he said, as he cut to the chase.
I am, I am,
said the Lamb;
I am, I am,
he was no sham.

In the beginning, I am just was,
some help this gives, it does, it does.

To hear I am was, speaks of a past,
like I am being the first and the last.

He's the Alpha and Omega in Greek,
the I am like no other - unique.

The I am to some is just strange business.
To others the I am just is, he's isness.

Love Lasts (1 Corinthians 13)

I may speak like no one around,
    persons enthralled, persons spellbound.

My speech may be like an angel's song,
    but without love, merely a gong.

Without love, no matter my speech,
    it will come off a terrible screech!

We're talking fingernails on a chalkboard,
    a nasty cacophony of discord.

If I preach with power
    for ten minutes or an hour;
        if I have all kinds of smarts,
            that impress others hearts;
                if I have faith to tell the hills to leap,
                    without love all is zilch, my talk is cheap.

If I give away all of my stuff,
    without love it won't be enough.

My pretentious ego, the way I boast,
    comes across smelly like burnt toast.

With patient love, humble, very kind,
    snottiness and control we will not find.

        Love does not brag,
            does not nag.
        Love does not sag,
            does not lag.
        Love is not being first in line.
        Love is not me, myself and mine.
        Love parties at what is right.
        Love observed is quite a sight.
        Love bears, believes, hopes all things;
            in harmony with others, love sings.

Tongues may go away, all kaputt,
    while love endures and stays put.

Prophesy and smarts will one day cease,
    they're only partial, only a piece.

God's full truth will be known
  when God's love for all is shown.

When I was a child, that's how I thought;
  at times I was wild, some wrongs I brought.

These days I have my adult pants on,
  my childish ways I have foregone.

Still we see things in a blur,
  and about much we are unsure.

The day will come when we see clearly,
  the way God sees and loves us dearly.

Until then, love, faith and hope rock;
  and love is numero uno—it is a lock!

www.ingramcontent.com/pod-product-compliance
Ingram Content Group UK Ltd.
Pitfield, Milton Keynes, MK11 3LW, UK
UKHW041919190726
13854UKWH00003B/1322